Selling Cars as a King's Kid

Stories of God's Guidance and Miracles on the Showroom Floor

Gaylord Thomas

Selling Cars as a King's Kid

Stories of God's Guidance and Miracles on the Showroom Floor

Gaylord Thomas

FiveStonePress
Romulus, Michigan

Selling Cars as a King's Kid:
Stories of God's Guidance and Miracles on the Showroom Floor
by Gaylord Thomas

ISBN 978-1-959547-09-9

For Worldwide Distribution, Printed in the U.S.A.

FiveStonePress
Every Book a Giant-Killer
An imprint of Supernatural Truth Productions, LLC
www.FiveStonePress.com

Contents

Foreword

By Rebecca Clark

I had the pleasure of working with Gaylord from 2003 to 2009 at Hines Park Ford in Michigan.

It's hard to talk about Gaylord without also saying "and Linda," because that's just how they are. They come as a pair.

Every day they arrived at work together in their beautiful Mustang convertible, often wearing matching baseball caps and coordinated outfits. They ate lunch together every day and were always laughing and smiling—not only at each other, but at everyone who crossed their path. I honestly can't remember either of them ever saying a bad word about anyone.

They took every opportunity to give God the glory for their personal and professional success.

Gaylord would jump at any chance to pray for someone or show them kindness—whether they were asking for it or didn't yet realize they needed it! Linda shared the same generous spirit. Around the dealership she was known as our "Dealership Mom." She was always looking for ways to help people, even making personalized Christmas ornaments by hand for every employee.

Gaylord has the best laugh and an unforgettable smile, and he made our office a better place to be. God has blessed Gaylord and Linda in many ways, and they have used those blessings like ripples in a pond—spreading kindness and encouragement to countless others.

In the car business it's rare for customers to become friends with their salesperson, and even rarer for those friendships to last years after retirement. Yet that's exactly what has happened for Gaylord. I am grateful for the years we worked together, and I treasure the annual visits we still make between Tennessee and Michigan to stay in touch.

So what does Gaylord love?

He loves the Lord, his wife, his family, the car business (which he still dreams about almost every night), and any opportunity to help others through the Lord.

My hope is that this book shows you who Gaylord truly is and continues his legacy of loving God and loving people.

Rebecca Clark
Friend, colleague, and fellow believer

Introduction

By Art Thomas

Dinnertime at my childhood home was rarely quiet. Dad would come home from work, Mom would set food on the table, and almost every night Dad had a new story to tell—another testimony about how God had helped him at work that day.

These are the stories I was raised on. I've probably heard each of them a hundred times or more, and many of them I remember hearing on the very day they happened.

But for me, these aren't just stories. I spent many hours at my dad's dealership—sometimes doing homework after school, sometimes watching TV in the customer lounge near the service department, and often telling jokes or showing off for the sales staff, who usually seemed happy for a little distraction in the middle of a long day.

I remember peeking into the General Sales Manager's office and seeing the board on the wall with every salesperson's name and tally marks showing how many cars they had sold that month. Dad's line of tallies was usually two to four times longer than anyone else's. In the same way, the shelf above his desk was always filled with awards for sales records and customer satisfaction—something made even more obvious when compared with the shelves above the other desks.

But while Dad displayed those awards to help build trust with customers, I never saw him rub his success in the noses of the other salespeople. Instead, he helped them whenever he could. He pointed them to Jesus and prayed for them. And when Dad's workload became too much for one person, Mom joined him at the dealership—not just helping with paperwork and other tasks but praying for people and sharing Jesus right alongside him. By the time Dad retired, the two of them had become like parents or grandparents to the rest of the staff.

Even though Dad worked on commission and always had plenty to do, I often watched him spend extra time praying with a customer or sharing a story about God's faithfulness.

Dad taught by example that while life is full of challenges, our God is bigger. Even when my mom and later he each faced cancer, he chose the path of thanksgiving and rejoicing, trusting his heavenly Father to come through in the end. And that's just what happened time and again.

In all of this, my dad lived out Jesus's words in Matthew 6:33. If we "seek first his kingdom and his righteousness," then "all these things will be given to you as well." In other words, if we put God and His mission first, He will take care of our needs. Yes, Dad became one of the top Ford salesmen in the country, but his life proved something even more important—he wasn't ultimately working for a dealership. He was working for God.

Today, about seventeen years after retiring from car sales, he's still working for God. He continues to love my mom, encourage his church, and share stories of God's faithfulness with almost everyone he meets. In fact, you may be reading this book because you just met him and he handed it to you!

I can assure you that every story in this book is true. And if you let these stories point you to the same Jesus my dad serves, you can enjoy your own adventures with the Lord. He loves to show favor to His kids.

Art Thomas
Founding Pastor of Roots Church, Canton, Michigan
Gaylord and Linda's youngest son

1

A Passion for Cars

A childhood pedal car sparks a lifelong dream.

Take delight in the LORD, and he will give you the desires of your heart (Psalm 37:4).

When I was 3 years old my parents gave me a maroon pedal car for my birthday. I loved that car so much that I even drove it on cold Michigan winter days. It gave me a love for cars. I drove it until I couldn't fit in it anymore.

I loved to build model cars as I got older, and my favorite was a '49 Buick where I snipped the center windshield post out of to make it look like a '50 Buick. I continued building many model cars out of various materials and made some from scratch out of wood.

In high school study hall, I designed and drew cars the entire hour. I often rode my bicycle down to Gorno Ford in Trenton, Michigan, to watch the salespeople with envy.

Every few years, my dad would take me to the showrooms when he would pick out a new car, and I loved watching how the salespeople handled each transaction. He would also ask for my input. For example, when he was ready to trade in his '55 Hudson Hornet, he asked me if he should buy a '57 Hornet. I told him that American Motors Corporation would be discontinuing the Hudson and he would be stuck with an orphan! I talked him into a beautiful '57 Chrysler Saratoga in robin-egg blue with a white top.

Yes, it was my dream to sell cars, but at 17, I did not think any dealerships would hire me.

After graduation, my sister, who worked as a secretary at the Ford glass house (headquarters), helped me land a job as a mail carrier at the Ford Motor Company. It was not a sales job, but it was at least at an automotive company. After that position, I moved to the Livonia Transmission plant. There I received many promotions, including the supervisor of payroll, which I enjoyed. I supervised a group of 7 people who were responsible for paying 2,000 hourly workers.

Then I learned I could move further up the ranks by taking a college accounting course at the University of Michigan Dearborn. This allowed me to be promoted to an accounting job where I was responsible for paying many vendors that did business with the Livonia Transmission plant. Other duties included payroll responsibilities for six other Ford plants.

I was making a very good living. It was regular pay plus yearly performance and cost of living raises. I loved each new job, even though it was not selling cars. But I couldn't escape that dream, and eventually the opportunity would present itself.

2

Stepping Out in Faith

Leaving a secure career to pursue the dream God placed in my heart.

"For I know the plans I have for you," declares the Lord, "plans to prosper you and not to harm you, plans to give you hope and a future" (Jeremiah 29:11).

In 1987, after I had been with Ford for 28 years, they gave me the "30-year Golden Handshake," which meant I could retire at the age of 45 and pursue the desire of my heart: selling cars. I wasn't 100% sure this was what I was supposed to do, so before I took the offer, I phoned three Ford dealerships to see if they would be interested in hiring someone like me. They all said, "Absolutely!"

Unfortunately, right after I retired, there was a downturn in the market. Since very few cars were being sold, there was no longer a need for extra salespeople—especially one with no experience. They read my resume and saw that I had an excellent work record at Ford and that I presented myself well, but any available job was taken by seasoned salespeople because they did not have to be trained.

Several months went by. We used some of our early-retirement money to put new carpeting and windows in our house, buy new furniture, and take motorhome trips to the Smoky Mountains. We had never experienced so much money all at one time, and I still had another lump-sum settlement coming in August of that year. It was truly exciting, until I reviewed our books after three months and discovered we weren't going to make it until the next settlement payment in August of '88.

I picked up the Detroit News and went right to the job ads for car salespeople.

One intrigued me, stating, "No sales experience necessary," but it was for a Buick dealer. I had been exclusively loyal to Ford (and talking down General Motors) my whole life, so I naturally wondered if this would be wrong. I was forgetting that I didn't owe Ford anything. I had given them an honest day's work for an honest day's pay. The Lord had put the food on my table.

So, that night I prayed and asked the Lord to tell me what to do—for some sort of inner feeling that it would be okay to work for GM.

Well, I got absolutely nothing.

The next morning I prayed the same way again, and this time I asked the Lord if it would be in His will for me to sell Buicks.

Again, I got nothing.

Then, as I walked across the bedroom floor, an audible voice said to me, "Who is your God?"

I said, "Lord Jesus, you are my God!"

The voice replied, "You have a job waiting for you at Buick."

I put on my best suit, grabbed my professional-looking briefcase and my resume, and off I went to Bill Cook Buick. I sat down in front of the General Manager, and he said, "You are just what we're looking for. Can you start tomorrow?"

Of course, I said yes.

The next day, I was with seven other newbies, and for five days we received the most wonderful training. Part of the training was to pose as customers at other dealerships. They told us to walk in and say we were just looking. In every case, the salesperson said, "Oh, you're just looking? Well, if you have any questions, come find me." I learned that they should have stuck with the potential customer to build rapport and become friends. Besides that, they also likely spent a couple days afterward feeling rejected. If you have not had rejection training and did not sell to the last two customers, you will feel too defeated to sell the third customer!

Did you know that price does not sell cars? What sells cars, or anything else for that matter, is *you*. You are the reason people buy your product. When customers walk into a dealership, they already have a good idea of what they want. In my 22 years, I never sold a car because it had one inch more legroom than a competitor or one more cubic foot of trunk space. Nor did I ever sell a car because of a low price. People buy cars because they like you. If you develop a friendship with them, they'll buy from you. If the bond is strong enough, even if they go to another dealer and are offered a lower price, they will come back to you. I almost never lost a sale because of price. I sold cars because the customers became my friends.

3

The Sign I Asked For

When I asked God for confirmation, the answer walked through the showroom door.

Whether you turn to the right or to the left, your ears will hear a voice behind you, saying, "This is the way; walk in it" (Isaiah 30:21).

Finally, it was time to sell a car! At around ten in the morning, a husband and wife walked in. That can make a sale much easier because if it is just the husband or wife, they may say, "I have to go talk this over with my spouse." I was all set and greeted them with a smile.

"Can I help you?" I asked.

The wife, Alice, answered, "No!" And she went to the next salesperson.

Oh my! Talk about rejection.

The next salesperson said to her, "Can I help you?"

Again, she said, "No!"

This trend continued until the last salesperson, at which point she remarked, "Don't you have a lady salesperson in here?"

The last salesman replied, "I'm sorry ma'am, we don't."

So, Alice barked in frustration, "Oh well. Then you'll do."

But he responded politely, "It's only right that I turn you back over to Mr. Thomas since he greeted you at the door".

Alice responded, "Well give me *somebody!*"

And so, there I was in my very first potential sales opportunity with a lady who was all upset.

When I asked them what they would like to drive, Alice responded, "A new '89 Buick Regal."

When I asked her husband for his driver's license, Alice pulled it out of *her purse!* Oh my. I had not been trained on something like this.

I was so nervous, I had to use both hands to get the car's key off the hook. They had trained me to go with the customer on test drives, so I got in the back seat while Alice got in the driver's seat and her husband in the passenger seat.

She looked over her shoulder and said, "I understand that if I hit something, this car is going to fold up like an accordion because it doesn't have a frame anymore."

I told her the frame is actually designed that way so that it will absorb the impact energy of the crash instead of your bones. The government had put out regulations to improve the safety of cars with this type of design.

Her husband looked up at her and calmly said, "He's right dear."

To which Alice responded, "Oh shut up."

That back-and-forth continued for the next ten minutes. Alice would ask me a question, to which I had the perfect answer, (because I was fresh out of automotive school), and every time her husband would tell her I was right, and Alice would tell him to shut up.

It was such a horrible experience that when I got back to the dealership, I wondered if I really wanted to sell cars! At that point, she started to beat me up on the price. I started at the sticker price as I was trained and went all the way down to $100 over invoice. After that point, the car could not go "over the curb," meaning we would not make anything on the sale. Now what would I do?

They taught us in training that if you can't sell your customer at $100 over invoice, then get up out of your chair, beat your head on the wall three times, sit back down, look the customer in the eye and say, "You have all the money I've got!" So that's what I did.

Alice said, "I'll take it."

Two days later I delivered her the car. This first sale was from the Lord because it made all the rest easy.

That same week, a shoe salesman who had gone through training with me—someone who didn't even want to sell cars and showed no enthusiasm—sold and delivered three cars. I couldn't help but think, *What am I doing at a dealership selling cars?* I started to wonder if I had really heard the Lord's voice.

The next Monday, I went into work early and sat at my desk in prayer. I said to the Lord, "I'm not so sure I'm in Your will to be here at this Buick dealer. Did I really hear Your voice? If so, I want a sign." I had never asked for a sign from the Lord in my life.

Five minutes later, after the doors to the showroom had opened, a gentlemen walked in and came straight to me. He said, "Hi, my name is

Michael Christ, spelled c-h-r-i-s-t. I'm a brother of the fella upstairs, and I'm here to buy a car."

I said, "Hallelujah! Let's pick one out."

He already had the exact car in mind and handed me the VIN number. It was a red four-door Buick LeSabre on the lot. His price was set due to General Motors employee-pricing discounts, and he was paying cash. He put a $100 bill down to hold the car and said he would pick it up the next day.

How's that for a sign?

It was the easiest sale of my life, and from then on, you couldn't stop me. I became their top salesman in the fourth month. Two of the new salespeople were fired and two quit, so I was left on the floor with three seasoned salespeople. Yet with no experience, I was out selling them. I love being a King's kid!

When you work for a car dealership as a salesperson, you get no salary. You only get paid if you sell a car and deliver it. Our son, Art, was three years old, and I was trusting the Lord that I could make a living selling cars. Wow, did He come through! The very first year, I doubled the salary I was getting at my Ford supervisor job, and in the fourth year of selling, I was making four times my old salary!

From the very first car I delivered, I started pre-setting three Christian radio stations on the dial, along with the secular stations. The Lord honored my ministry, as you will hear in the upcoming stories.

Soon after, a customer came into the dealership looking like a homeless man. His jeans were torn, his shirt was dirty, and he had a two-day beard. But God is no respecter of persons. I walked up to him and asked if I could help him. He told me he wanted to test drive the Buick Electra, so I did the standard protocol of making a copy of his license and pulling up a new '89 Electra. He drove it for fifteen minutes and then came back and told me he would like to buy it. His price was already determined through a special GM program, leaving no room for negotiation. I also sold him a five-year warranty and interior/exterior protection.

The next day, I was taken aback when the same man came in to pick up his car—clean shaven and wearing an expensive suit. I almost didn't recognize him.

He said, "Mr. Thomas. I want to tell you why I bought this car from you. I dressed like a bum yesterday on purpose to see how I would be treated. I went to three Buick dealerships, and you were the only one to wait on me. You even addressed me as 'Sir!' I am a doctor at St. Mary's hospital."

I told him how all four of my kids were born there.

When you have the Lord's favor, you can just relax and know you are going to sell to almost everyone you talk to.

The next day, I lost a customer to Mercury because the Buick didn't have childproof locks on the rear doors. The following day, I lost a sale to Ford because the Buick had cruise control on the wiper stalk instead of the steering wheel.

Was the Lord telling me it was time to move to a Ford dealership?

4

My Move to Ford

How God used an unexpected conversation to guide my next step.

See, I am doing a new thing! Now it springs up; do you not perceive it? I am making a way in the wilderness and streams in the wasteland (Isaiah 43:19).

I had been at Bill Cook Buick for nine months and was the top salesperson for six of those months. I realized I now had enough credentials to approach a Ford dealership. I called up Ford headquarters and asked which dealership had the best service record. I was happily surprised that it was a small dealership six miles from my house. So, I updated my resume, wrote a cover letter, and sent it off to McDonald Ford in Northville.

Three days later, I followed up with a phone call to their General Manager, and he said he had received my resume but did not have a sales position available. I pressed him, saying I lived just five miles from the dealership, and he asked if I could come in for an interview.

At my Buick dealership, they gave their top salesperson an Electra to drive. So, I drove my new Buick Electra to the McDonald Ford showroom. The General Manager watched me pull up and, clearly flustered, told me that he did not give his sales staff a beautiful car like I was driving. I told him I didn't need a demo and that I had two Ford models at home. I said, "I'm here to sell cars."

He walked me to his office and started to go over the pay plan. As he started explaining his complicated formula, I stopped him and asked, "Do you pay all of your salespeople the same rate no matter how long they have been here?"

"Yes," he replied.

"Fine," I said, "I will come in here and make a living for you and for me, or I will be out of here."

He asked if I could start in five days.

Oh wow! I was hired! As I drove my Electra back to the Buick dealership, that strong sign the Lord had given me through Michael Christ came to me again, but I still wanted to confirm it with the Lord.

I was a king at Buick. I was loved, and I could do no wrong. I also loved working there, so I asked the Lord, "If it is truly Your will, would You give me another sign about moving to McDonald Ford?"

Three hours later, a customer walked into Bill Cook and asked if we had any Electras. We had 20, so we walked onto the new car lot, and the first car we came to was painted in rose beige. He said, "That's the car I want," and, thanks to a prearranged program, the price was fixed and non-negotiable. He gave me $100 to hold the car for pick-up the next day. This was the second easiest sale of my life.

As we sat down at my desk, he started writing his deposit check but stopped in the middle. "Mr. Thomas, I've got to ask you something. Are you thinking of leaving?"

That was surprising. So, I inquired why he would ask.

"I just want to make sure you'll still be here if I have a problem with this car."

I obviously could not tell him I was considering leaving, so I told him before he took delivery of his new vehicle, I would walk him into the Service Department and introduce him to the Service Manager, and they would be on a first-name basis.

When he finished writing the check, I asked him again why he was so worried that I might be leaving Bill Cook Buick.

He replied, "Mr. Thomas, I don't mean to scare you, but everytime I buy a car, the salesperson seems to leave five days later."

As you can imagine, I took that as quite a sign. I walked over to the General Manager. He took one look at me and said, "You're leaving me, aren't you? I knew you would leave me some day."

I told him yes and that I was going to McDonald Ford in Northville. He told me that it was a good dealership. I stayed on until the end of the week and worked hard for him selling three more Buicks for a total of eighteen that month.

5

The Desk with the Clock

A forgotten prayer comes true seventeen years later.

"This vision is for a future time. It describes the end, and it will be fulfilled. If it seems slow in coming, wait patiently, for it will surely take place. It will not be delayed" (Habakkuk 2:3).

On my first day at the McDonald Ford, I asked where my desk would be. The General Manager walked me over to the only empty desk on the showroom floor.

The first thing I did was say a prayer thanking God that He had given me this wonderful opportunity to sell Ford vehicles. I opened my eyes to become familiar with my surroundings and noticed a round, bright spot on the wall above my desk where a clock had once hung. At that moment, I remembered a prophetic statement I made years prior.

At that time, my wife, Linda, and I had purchased a new 1973 Ford pick-up truck from the salesperson who sat at that very same desk. I remembered that after I signed the paperwork for the truck and walked outside, I turned to Linda and said, "Someday, I'm going to realize my dream and sell cars from this building and *from that very desk with the clock over it!*"

This was something that I had totally forgotten about. I picked this store to sell cars because Ford headquarters told me they had the best repair service in the whole Detroit area. In fact, back in 1973, it was even under a different dealership name. I love being a King's kid!

After I had been at McDonald Ford for a week, I went back to Bill Cook Buick to pick up my commission check. As I walked back to my car, a customer who I had only met once pulled up to my car and asked if I was going for lunch. I told him if he wanted to buy a Buick from me, he would have to see another salesperson because I had moved to McDonald Ford in Northville. He said, "Ford vehicles are good too," and an hour later he walked into McDonald Ford and bought a Tempo from me.

It is so fun living and walking with the Lord while doing the desire of your heart.

6

The Wrong Lincoln

The day my customer drove off in the dealership owner's brand-new car.

And we know that in all things God works for the good of those who love him, who have been called according to his purpose (Romans 8:29).

After nine months of selling Buicks, I was now two weeks into my new position at McDonald Ford. I was already outselling the entire sales staff. I couldn't seem to do anything wrong.

Or could I?

I phoned my insurance agent and informed him where I was working in case he needed a car immediately for a client. He asked if I had any two-year-old Lincolns on the used car lot. I told him no, but I could have my dealer get one from auction. I just needed to know what color he would like.

He answered, "Dark blue with a black vinyl top and blue leather interior."

I relayed this information to the Used Car Sales Manager, and he found one the very next day! My insurance agent brought in his wife that evening for a test drive.

I was unaware that Mr. McDonald, my dealership's owner, had just pulled up in his new dark blue Lincoln with a black vinyl top and only 10 miles on the odometer. He parked in the delivery isle, right in front of the identical used dark blue Lincoln we had found. Both cars had the keys in the ignition.

Mr. McDonald, whom I had never met, stood at the foot of the driveway as my insurance agent and his wife drove off in his brand-new Lincoln! I had not noticed the used vehicle behind it.

The General Manager who was standing next to him came running over to my desk. His face was beet-red as he asked me if I had just put my customers in a dark blue Lincoln.

"Yes," I replied with a big smile.

Then he told me what had happened and how upset Mr. McDonald was.

It looked like my career at McDonald Ford had just ended!

During my first week, I was told the owner never spoke to salespeople. But the Lord spoke to me and told me to introduce myself to Mr. McDonald and let him know that I had enjoyed working for him. I bravely walked up to him, shook his hand, and said, "Hi Mr. McDonald, I'm Gaylord Thomas, the new kid on the block. I just put my customers in your new Lincoln. I'm very sorry, and I want you to know that it has been a pleasure working for you!"

He laughed and laughed.

Soon my customers were back from their test drive and asked if I had put them in the wrong car, likely noticing the low odometer reading.

I had them take another test drive in the two-year-old Lincoln, and it drove exactly like the new one, so they bought it.

From then on, Mr. McDonald spoke to me on a daily basis. Yes, when you are carrying the Lord in your heart, He can direct you in everything you do.

7

The Kindness Bonus

A simple act of kindness turns into an unexpected blessing.

"Truly I tell you, whatever you did for one of the least of these brothers and sisters of mine, you did for me" (Matthew 25:40).

It was a very busy Thursday evening at the Ford dealership, with lots of customers to assist. The Lord directed me to Jimmy—a young man with special needs. He wanted to buy a car but only had $1,000 to put down and was interested in a Ranger truck.

I asked him where he worked, and he told me he was a mail clerk at the main AAA insurance office. I took the opportunity to build our relationship, telling him that I started at Ford as a mail clerk. From that moment on, he was my friend. I pulled up a new Ranger truck for a test drive, and off he went.

While he was on the test drive, the truck manager came over and told me that every salesperson in there had waited on this young man and that he would never be able to buy a new car or truck because of his financial situation and his special needs.

I reminded the manager that Jimmy drove a car to the dealership and has a job. Right then the Lord brought to my mind the time I had waited on the man who looked homeless and very poor. (The man had actually been a doctor but dressed like a homeless man and bought the car from me because I was kind and treated him as a person.)

When the young man came back from his test drive, I gave him the monthly payment he would have with his down payment, but it was still more money than he could afford. He was on a pre-arranged price plan because his dad worked at Ford, so there was no room for negotiation. I told him that as soon as he saved up enough money, he should come see me again. When he left, the salespeople teased me for waiting on him since it was such a busy night.

Three weeks later, Ford introduced a new inexpensive car called the Festiva. I immediately phoned Jimmy, and he rushed down to the dealership. He test drove the Festiva and loved it. I gave him the price, and he went home to discuss it with his parents. The next day, his father brought him to the dealership. He walked over to me and said, "I understand that you have spent a lot of time with my son, and he would like to buy a new Festiva from you."

You might think the story ends there, but it gets better. The next day, when delivering the car, the salespeople were teasing me again because the Festiva was the lowest commission you could make on a deal. But then we were all called into the Sales Manager's office for an announcement from Ford that any salesperson selling a Festiva that month would receive a bonus check for $100.

I had made such a friendship with Jimmy that every month he would tell me how many miles he had on the car and how wonderful the gas mileage was.

Shortly after, he called from the hospital. He was okay, but he had been rear ended on the expressway, and his car was totaled. But he wanted a new Festiva—in red. The following day, I delivered his new red Festiva, and I received another $100 bonus!

8

Never Judge the Customer

Why you should never assume who can—or cannot—buy a car.

"The Lord does not look at the things people look at. People look at the outward appearance, but the Lord looks at the heart" (1 Samuel 16:7).

A friend of mine, who had an office job at Ford, sent his janitor, Tom, to me. Tom had some cognitive issues, speech difficulties, and he was hard of hearing. My friend from Ford had told me that Tom loved to use his metal detector to hunt for treasure, so I asked him about it when he visited the dealership, and we became friends.

He loved telling me about his hobby and the places he would travel with his mom, whom he lived with. He would go on treasure hunts, even as far as Virginia.

After some more small talk, he decided he wanted the beautiful new Eddie Bauer Aerostar with special fiberglass running boards, which we had just put on the showroom floor.

Suddenly, the Sales Manager called me into his office and yelled, "Throw that drunk out! And look how he is dressed. He can't afford anything!"

I replied, "Just give me three more minutes to sign the buyer's order because he is buying that expensive Eddie Bauer Aerostar with an added extra protection package and an extended warranty."

Tom did buy the vehicle, and a few months later, he brought his mom. She purchased a new Taurus.

I love being a King's kid!

9

Sign Them Up Before They Die

A routine delivery becomes one of the most unforgettable moments of my career.

"My flesh and my heart may fail, but God is the strength of my heart and my portion forever" (Psalm 73:26).

I was in my second year of selling cars at McDonald Ford. The staff didn't like me because I was too energetic while living my dream. Their monthly goals were ten cars a month, and I was always in the twenties or thirties.

One morning, an older couple came in and purchased a new '90 Taurus. They planned to pick it up the next morning at 10:00 a.m. and would pay in cash. On the morning of delivery, the wife called to tell me they would be a little late because her husband was experiencing chest pains, and they were going to stop by the doctor's office on the way. I told her we could complete the delivery another day, but she said her husband was insistent on getting it out of the way.

They arrived at 10:30am, and their daughter was driving them with the dad in the back seat. They helped him into the showroom, and I asked how he was doing. He said the doctor had told him to go to the hospital immediately, but he wanted to finish the deal.

I told him we could sign all the paperwork, he could go to the hospital, and then I would instruct his wife on the controls and features of the new car later in the day. He liked that idea, and we all sat at my desk as I explained the paperwork.

There were twenty-one signatures, and after he signed number twenty, he asked if there were any more.

"Just one," I told him.

As soon as he signed it, he whispered to his daughter, "Call 911."

His wife handed me the cash for the car, and I had to take it to the cashier in the service area.

As I was out of the showroom area, my wife, Linda, stopped by for a visit and saw all the emergency vehicles. There was no place to park. She became concerned when it occurred to her that maybe I was the patient, so she parked across the street and walked in, only to see five salespeople standing in line, and I wasn't one of them. The man laying on the floor near my desk was wearing dark blue pants like mine, and she could only see his legs sticking out.

As I walked into the showroom with the money receipt, I spotted Linda, and she was as white as a sheet. I tapped her on the shoulder and asked her if watching the paramedics working on my customer was bothering her.

"I thought it was you!"

Once he was in the ambulance, they stabilized him for 30 minutes before they pulled away.

Around 5:00 p.m., his wife and daughter came back to pick up the new car. Her husband had just had a quadruple bypass and was doing fine.

From then on, the sales staff had a new nickname for me; "Sign-them-up-before-they-die Gaylord."

10

The Quest for 300 Cars

The incredible story of how car number 300 arrived at the perfect moment.

But as for you, be strong and do not give up, for your work will be rewarded (2 Chronicles 15:7).

If you are doing your best to meet your job goals and always looking for opportunities to share the Lord, can you expect God to make what seems impossible happen? Well, let me build your faith.

It was only my second year at the McDonald Ford, and I was on track to become the first salesperson in the dealership to become a Grand Master of Sales, which would mean I met the goal of selling 300 cars in a calendar year. This total could not include fleet sales and required only favorable customer feedback. At that time in Michigan, there were only twenty-five people who had ever achieved this.

It was December 29—the last full day of selling, since the next day would be only a half day. I had sold 299 cars for the year and needed to deliver only one more to become a Grand Master. This recognition came with $500 from Ford headquarters, a gold Ford ring valued at $500, and a large wooden plaque engraved with my name.

The temperature was below freezing, and most people don't purchase cars the week after Christmas. They are busy planning New Years Eve parties, and they had just spent a lot on Christmas.

It was 10:30 a.m., and I had just delivered car 299. Mr. McDonald called every hour to see if I sold and delivered number 300. He wanted to brag to his friends that he had a Grand Master!

The sales staff did not want me to get the 300th deal because they were jealous. They were ready with their fingers on the phone button in case a new car call came in. They were also watching the front doors of the dealership like hawks.

I prayed that if the Lord wanted me to become a Grand Master, he would have to provide the customer. I then organized the paperwork from sale number 299, placed it in the deal jacket, and walked to the back of the office for finalization.

As I was crossing the showroom floor, I saw a truck driver come in the front door. We often had truck drivers stop at our dealership, asking for directions because they didn't realize that the road continued on after merging with another road for one block. The other salespeople did not think this was a potential sale—they thought he was lost. I too thought he wanted directions, so I asked if I could help him while still walking by.

He replied, "Do you have any leftover Aerostars?"

I heard several salespeople groan from their desks. I walked him over to the side glass doors and pointed to 20 of them in the front row.

He then stated, "You're going to think I'm crazy, but I was just driving my eighteen-wheeler down the road when an audible voice told me that you have a better deal for me than I have at another Ford dealership.

I asked him if he had any exclusive pricing available through a company program, and he did. I couldn't help him there.

I then asked if he had a vehicle to trade in, which he did. So, I told him that I did have a better deal for him, and he said he would come back at 7:00 p.m.

There were no other phone or walk-in customers the rest of the day.

At 7:00 p.m., he drove in with his 5-year-old Ford Country Wagon with old fashioned simulated wood siding. I was really hoping for a newer car. I took it over to the used car manager and had him appraise the car. Once back in the show room, I showed it to the customer, and he replied, "Wow! That's $500 better than I had at another dealer!"

I grabbed a buyer's form and started to write up the deal.

He stopped me and said, "I have been dealing with the same salesperson for ten years. Don't you think that the other dealer will match this?"

I replied, "Absolutely. Take this paperwork over to your past dealer, and I'm sure they will match it. I'm surprised, however, you don't want to buy it from me. The other dealer didn't give you the best price right away. I have been very honest with you and would like to have you as my friend."

Then I heard the Lord's voice say, "Deposit!"

I asked, "Do you maybe have a deposit over there at the other dealer?"

He replied, "Yes I do. $50."

I told him that if he didn't get his deposit back, I would give it to him myself.

He replied, "You have a deal!"

The next day—the last day we were open for the year—I delivered number 300!

As my customer was leaving in his new Aerostar, I told him how his sale had made me a Grand Master and how he was an answer to prayer. I also told him that he had heard the Lord's voice as he came upon our dealership.

He was very excited and told me that Saturday he was scheduled to speak at a men's breakfast at his church, and this gave him the perfect material of how he helped a fellow Christian that week.

I called him up after a week to see how he liked his new vehicle, and he was very happy.

… and he did get his $50 deposit back.

11

The Husband-and-Wife Team

How working together with Linda made the job even more special.

"Two are better than one, because they have a good return for their labor: If either of them falls down, one can help the other up" (Ecclesiastes 4:9–10).

In my third year at the Ford dealership, I was receiving so many referrals that it was getting difficult to give full attention to all my customers. I already had my wife Linda picking up my dealer trades, and she had become familiar with the procedures of selling cars.

So, I asked management for a desk and phone for her, and they agreed. We became known as the husband-and-wife team. Our customers loved having her there to help them pick out a new car. While I was writing up a sale for one customer, she could be showing another customer a vehicle.

She was not allowed to wait on a new customer walking in unless they asked for me. After that, she could show them cars and put them on test drives. She also took the pressure off by entertaining my customers' kids while I sold and delivered cars.

One evening, a father brought in his lease car to turn in, and he had his two kids with him—ages seven and nine. He got so excited picking up his new lease vehicle that he left his kids with Linda!

This was before cell phones were common, so I had to wait. I knew he had about a 20-minute drive home. I waited until I thought he would be home and then called his home to offer to bring the children home for him. But his wife answered and said she had just turned her husband around to come pick up the kids.

I'll bet that he never lived down—trading in his kids for a new car!

Our dealer was only open five days a week, yet Linda and I were always selling over and above 350 a year. One year, we even hit 400! We once had nine deliveries in a single day, and we worked it out so that no customer had any wait time.

Most days, we went to lunch together, and it was wonderful having my best friend at my side. It was a Christian testimony to the staff and our customers how well we worked together. She was such a blessing.

12

A Crash Course in Grace

When a test drive crashed through the showroom window.

You will keep in perfect peace those whose minds are steadfast, because they trust in you (Isaiah 26:3).

One day, Linda and I had just come back from lunch. An older couple came into the dealership to return a lease from another dealer. They wanted to purchase their next vehicle closer to their new apartment, which was just five miles away.

The man told me that he had MS and, while he could get around with his walker, he may need a wheelchair in the future. He had been thinking of a

Focus Wagon because it would be easier for his wife to place the chair in the back than lifting it into another Taurus, which was their current vehicle.

As Linda pulled up a Ford Focus, I asked who was going to test drive. The wife said that her husband did all the driving.

His walker had wheels and hand brakes, and as he went out the door, he tripped on the carpet and almost fell! I couldn't stop him from driving since he had a valid driver's license, but as they drove away, I was a little nervous.

Meanwhile, my phone was ringing with another lease customer. As I was taking care of them, I heard a tremendous crash.

My Linda screamed, "Your customer just drove the Focus through the showroom window!"

I looked up, and the car was jammed against the window frame, which was stopping the car from coming all the way in. The front tires were still at full throttle, spinning a hole in the showroom carpet.

I ran over and helped his wife out of the passenger seat, and she needed immediate medical attention. Her heart had gone into atrial fibrillation, and she was having trouble breathing. Whether that was before or after the crash, I am not sure. We called 911, and EMS was on their way.

When the police arrived, we had to get the driver out of the car. He had apparently hit the accelerator instead of the brake as he pulled into the dealership with his new wide shoes.

The policeman got him over the console gearshift and out the passenger door. As he walked him around the car, he motioned for the policeman to stop so he could pull his walker out of the rear door.

As the driver opened up his walker and shuffled away, I smiled at the policeman, and he did everything he could not to laugh.

They both went to the hospital in an ambulance, and later that afternoon, they came back to pick up their old car.

The next day, I called them to see how they were doing. The husband replied, "We are both just fine. We have decided to lease another Taurus… And I don't need to test drive it!"

I kept in touch with these people, and Linda and I even visited them at their apartment. You see, even though we had already delivered their new Tarus, it was important to Linda and me that they knew there were no hard feelings for crashing into our dealership.

And there is more to this story. On the day of the crash, Ford Motor Company's building inspector was there, grading us on the looks of the dealership. Everything had to be perfectly in order for us to pass and receive the Blue Oval Award.

For weeks, we'd had numerous carpet cleaners come to try and remove the oil stains out of the carpeting. It would temporarily work, but after a day or two, the oil would seep back in. We were sure we would loose our Blue Oval Award. We had passed every other criteria. All that remained was this review of our carpeting.

The jealous sales staff were excited that maybe something was finally going to be blamed on me. However, the inspector took one look at the carpeting and said, "With all that glass on it, I really can't judge it, so I will just give you a pass. You have your Blue Oval Award!"

Before closing that day, a wood replacement for the missing window was in place, all three wrecked cars were in the body shop. Within two weeks, everything was back in proper order.

I love being a King's kid! The Lord kept me calm throughout the whole experience, telling me everything was going to be just fine.

13

Helping Customers, One Lease at a Time

How a new idea transformed my sales career.

"Let us not become weary in doing good, for at the proper time we will reap a harvest if we do not give up" (Galatians 6:9).

In 1990, Ford had all their salespeople attend a seminar on leasing. With my background in accounting, I immediately saw the light: If my customers leased their vehicles, then in two years, I would have a guaranteed clientele.

Many of my customers would buy new cars from me every few years already. I couldn't wait to present leasing as an option. If explained correctly, leasing made a whole lot of sense to most of my customers who simply wanted a reliable vehicle for a local commute.

I had to learn how to use a small, hand-held computer, and lease deals took me an extra ten minutes. The other salespeople thought I was foolish spending extra time presenting a lease to every customer. That is, until two years later, when they saw all these same customers coming back to me for another new car. The extra time was worth it.

Thanks to the consistent repeat business, I ranked among the top ten Ford salespeople for leasing in the entire United States! With the Lord's help, the 300 to 400 cars I delivered each year were mostly two-year leases.

In one case, a lady walked into McDonald Ford and told me she just walked out of another dealership because the salesperson tried to push a lease on her. She said, "Don't talk to me about a lease!" So, I sold her a new Taurus.

After we finished the paperwork, she told me that she just made the last payment on her six-year-old car. I replied, "Oh no! And all this time, you could have had three new cars with a lower payment each month and never have had any car repairs or purchased new tires! All you would have had extra were oil changes."

She replied, "Talk to me about a lease."

It took me ten minutes to change her sale to a lease.

Another time a man in his late eighties walked into the dealership to purchase a new Taurus. They taught us in leasing school not to present a lease to a person over seventy. They said you could lose their next purchase. Of course, that didn't stop me.

I sold him the car, and he told me he would pick it up the next day and pay cash. When he was about to leave, I said to him, "I really don't need for you to take $21,000 out of the bank tomorrow. I will only need $7,000 of it, and you can leave the other $14,000 in the bank for two years. Can you make any money by leaving $14,000 in the bank for 2 years?"

"You're darn right, I can!" he said.

I replied, "Great. You leave your money there, and when you come back in two years, I will only need another $7,000, and I'll take your two-year-old car back and give you a brand new one."

He asked, "What kind of a program is this?"

I told him it was called a prepaid lease and that there were no monthly payments.

He replied, "Sign me up!"

The next day, he handed me his $7,000 check and said, "Mr. Thomas, this prepaid lease works perfect for me. I'm not planning on living more than two more years, and if I die, my kids will be able to have the money in the bank and not have to worry about selling the car."

In every car I sold, I continued the practice of pre-setting three Christian radio stations among all the secular ones. One of Linda's responsibilities was to drive each turned-in lease vehicle to a special spot for pickup in back of the building, and many times one of the Christian stations would be playing.

14

The Windstar Miracle

When a customer asked for the impossible—
and God provided.

"If you believe, you will receive whatever you ask for in prayer" (Matthew 21:22).

It was a beautiful sunny day at the dealership, and I had four deliveries to get ready. The paperwork was proceeding at a normal pace, and things were looking good.

Then, a lady walked in and was greeted by the General Sales Manager. I heard her tell the manager that she had just come from another Ford dealer and that the salesperson knew nothing about the new Windstar that had just come out.

I turned to Linda and told her, "I hope he doesn't bring her to me!" I was trying to make sure all my deliveries that day were perfect for the new customers, and this woman seemed like she might take a lot of time. Linda told me not to worry because she would check on my deliveries.

My sales manager walked her over to my desk and introduced us. She sat down and asked me four questions about the new Windstar, and the Lord helped me remember the correct answers.

I needed to go finish the paperwork for the four deliveries, so I said to her, "I overheard you say that you have already had a test drive at another dealer, but perhaps you would like my wife to pull up one for you so that you could take a longer test drive by yourself."

She thought that would be wonderful, so I had Linda pull up the nicest Eddie Bauer Windstar package for her. This gave me twenty minutes to get my paperwork in order.

When she came back, she said to me, "You're a born-again Christian, aren't you?"

"Yes," I replied.

She said, "Well, I want to buy my new Windstar from you!" She told me she wanted the Eddie Bauer in Mocha Frost with a trailer tow, air bags over the rear springs, leather seats, and a digital dash. I had never seen any vehicle equipped like that. As I opened my mouth to tell her I didn't think that such a Windstar even existed, out came, "No problem. I'll have it here tomorrow!"

I couldn't believe I had said that.

She remarked, "If you do that, I will bring my husband in to meet you, because that would make you the greatest salesperson in the whole world!"

At that moment, my manager drove up with his new Crown Victoria demo in Medium Willow Green. My customer asked, "What beautiful color is that?"

"Medium Willow Green," I answered, "and that color will be on the bottom portion of the Eddie Bower Windstar you just bought."

After she left, I put all the specs into the computer and, in a 100-mile radius, only one car was found, and that dealer was receiving the car that very day, fresh off the truck. Typically, a dealer will not trade a new car to a dealership more than twenty miles away because that means the return vehicle will have many additional miles on it. This dealer was in Grand Rapids, Michigan, which was about 100 miles away. I figured there was no chance, but it was the only one in the region, so I had to try.

I called the dealership and asked for the General Manager. "Hello. This is Gaylord Thomas at McDonald Ford."

He answered immediately and enthusiastically, "Did you say Gaylord Thomas from McDonald Ford?"

"Yes!" I replied.

He asked, "What can I do for you, sir?"

I gave him the rundown and told him what car I was looking for. He said they were just backing that unit off the truck, and if I could get my manager to agree to trade a Taurus Country Squire Wagon—which he had asked my manager for ten minutes prior—he would personally drive the Windstar to me!

Three hours later, I had my Windstar.

I called my customer and told her I would have it ready the next day at 10:30 a.m.

She couldn't believe it, and neither could I.

The next morning, Linda and I were cleaning the door jams on the car, and I asked Linda, "What color did she say she wanted?"

Linda replied, "Mocha Frost."

Then I said, "Why are we wiping down Medium Willow Green?"

Oh no! I had the wrong color!

I have sold customers a car that was missing a sunroof that they wanted, but color was usually more important.

As we walked back into the dealership, my customer and her husband drove up. I greeted her with a Christian hug and told her I was so sorry but had searched the wrong color.

She said, "Let's take a look at it." She walked all the way around the vehicle and said, "Mr. Thomas, I have a confession to make. I woke up this morning and asked God to change the color to Medium Willow Green!"

15

The Pink Paisley Taurus

Why the right relationship with customers always matters.

And let us not grow weary of doing good, for in due season we will reap, if we do not give up (Galatians 6:9).

My customer, Nancy, and her husband came in to renew their two-year lease. Nancy knew what she wanted since she had seen a new Taurus at another dealer. It was black with a pink paisley interior. She had already sat in it and wondered if I could get that car.

She could have just bought the car at the other dealership, but this shows again how important it is to be a friend to your customers. I told her Linda and I would pick it up the next day and have it ready by 7:00 p.m.

The following evening, it was all ready. The paperwork was complete, and the car was polished and ready for delivery. As they walked in, there was an excitement in both of them. I told her that before she signed the paperwork, she should sit in it one more time to make sure it was exactly what she wanted.

I walked them out to the delivery row where they commented how beautiful it looked. I opened the driver's door, and Nancy sat down and closed it. As I chatted with her husband, I glanced over and saw that she was crying. I asked her what was wrong, and she said, "I can't stand the pink paisley interior, even though I liked it the other night."

I told her that I would get her a black Taurus with a solid gray interior. She could not believe how nice I was about it, but I told her all I had to do was type up the new paperwork. I also told her that Ford got so many complaints in the first month for the pink paisley that they changed all of them to a solid color. We went to my desk and finished the paperwork.

As they were leaving, another previous customer came rushing into the dealership.

"Is that beautiful black Taurus with the gorgeous pink paisley interior available?"

"Absolutely," I replied.

All I had to do was type up the new paperwork, and away they went. Instead of having to go to management and undo a deal, I could sell another vehicle.

I love being a King's kid!

16

Guided by Grace: The Move to Hines Park

Praying for direction when one chapter of life comes to an end.

"Trust in the Lord with all your heart and lean not on your own understanding; in all your ways submit to him, and he will make your paths straight" (Proverbs 3:5–6).

After sixteen years of selling cars at McDonald Ford, there were rumors floating around that we were going out of business. This was largely due to the economic downturn and cultural worries following the events of September 11, 2001, which had people holding onto their money instead of making large purchases.

A week before that event, Mr. McDonald had taken delivery of approximately twenty-five Tracker

Trucks for our rental shop. That business bottomed out and made no money at all.

Ford Credit came in one morning and announced that our dealership was "out of trust." They seized control of all the new-car inventory, and this made it difficult to sell or even show vehicles without their involvement. Cashflow became a serious problem, and sufficient funds were necessary when delivering a car. Trades were all but impossible. A new owner of our dealership kept reassuring us and dismissing rumors, but I finally called Ford Motor headquarters, and they confirmed what I had feared—McDonald Ford was on its way out.

Other dealers started calling to see if I was interested in joining their sales team. It was fun being wanted, and my phone was ringing every day with crazy offers. However, I knew that all these dealers were not interested in Linda and me; they were only interested in getting our customer file. After all, none of these managers had ever invited Linda and me out for lunch. They knew us only from dealer trades and our Grand Master records, which were available through Ford.

It made most sense to move to the dealer closest to my home or closest for my customers. But every morning, I would start my day by asking the Lord where he wanted us to go. Linda and I would pray, "Lord, we have five dealers wanting us to work for them. Give us a sign where we should go."

Early one morning, as I parked at the dealership, a salesman who often looked after Linda and me when we were at lunch or on vacation pulled in at the same time. I lived only ten minutes away, while he commuted an hour, so that had never happened before.

He said, "Gaylord, wait up! I want you to know that I got hired at another dealership over the weekend!"

"Where?" I inquired.

There were dealers right by his house on the east side of Detroit, yet he had chosen one on the west side, an hour drive away.

So, I asked him why he would go there, and he told me that years ago, he had worked for the General Manager and that he was a real nice guy. Then he offered to call the General Manager up and ask him if he would like to have the Grand Master.

Five minutes later, I was being offered a job at a Ford dealership I had not considered.

It was 45 minutes from my house, and many of my customers would be passing one or two Ford dealerships to get there. Also, this was not one of the dealers offering me gifts to come. I told the General Manager, Robert, that I would come over for an interview the morning.

Robert greeted me with excitement in his step and had me sit down for a closed-door meeting. I decided that I was going to tell him many of the stories that you are reading in this book to see how he reacted to them. Robert was on the edge of his seat and egged me on for more. He also told me that Linda and I could openly pray with our customers on the showroom floor. Then he asked, "When can you and Linda start?"

I told him that the Lord hadn't told me which dealer to go to and that I would continue to pray for an answer.

The next day, a previous customer called to lease a new Explorer. He wanted a change from his current white vehicle to a new silver one with a matching leather interior and a moon roof. He lived a fair distance away and had to pass three Ford dealers just to buy from me. This would be his seventh vehicle from Linda and me.

I explained the dealership's financial situation and how we could not provide an immediate test drive, but we still went across the street and picked one out. We had twenty Explorers, but none that were silver with a moon roof. We did find one with a dark blue exterior, dark blue leather interior, and a moon roof. He said he would take that one.

Here is where the Lord came into the sale. Most salespeople would go back to the showroom and write up the sale. But I did not do that. I remembered how this customer and his wife would spend their winters in Florida.

"Don't you guys go to Florida for three months every winter?"

"Yes, every year," he said.

"Well, you should have white, silver, or gold. This dark blue is going to be too hot. I will find you a silver one."

They told me they did not want to be any trouble. I pointed out that McDonald Ford was going out of business, and we could not do any trades. I said they would likely find the unit in a light color at Hines Park Ford, and if I wasn't working there by Monday, I would find a salesperson to deliver it to them.

"You mean that beautiful new dealership we passed on the way here?"

I told them yes.

They started jumping up and down and said, "We want to be your first sale!"

So, I walked them to their car and put out a search for the silver Explorer. In a 100-mile radius, there was only one, and where do you think it was? I'm sure you have guessed correctly: Hines Park Ford.

So, I called up Robert—the General Manager I had interviewed with the day before. I asked if the silver Explorer was available.

He answered, "Yes. Would you like me call to your manager and make the trade?"

I said, "No. Just get it ready for delivery on Monday morning for me to deliver to my customer as my first sale working for you."

He replied, "You just made my day!"

Wow. This answer was really from the Lord. We ended up working at Hines Park Ford until we retired in 2009, and we were liked by everyone. We had so much fun that it was very hard to eventually leave.

17

The Power of Relationships

How a local bike shop owner became my easiest sale of the year.

Dear friends, let us love one another, for love comes from God (1 John 4:7).

In 2015, our dealership finally received a new Ford Transit Connect Window Van to sell. At lunch, Linda and I jumped in it for a test drive. The owner of Hines Park was standing on the sidewalk as we were getting in and said, "Are you going to sell that, Gaylord?"

I told him, "Absolutely!"

What he didn't know was that the owner of the local South Lyon Bike Shop had told me the previous year that if I ever got one in, he would most likely buy it because it would be ideal to transport bikes. I had purchased five new bikes from him in the past two years, and his wife had purchased a new car from me.

As we pulled up to the bike shop, I ran in and asked the owner to grab a bike with high handlebars. As we approached the van, Linda opened the two rear cargo doors, and he was able to place the bike right in without taking off the handlebars.

"Sold! Have it ready for tomorrow," he said.

You couldn't wipe the smiles off our faces. As we drove to the dealership, the owner was still standing there. This had to be the Lord orchestrating this.

He said, "Well, did you sell it?"

I told him with a big smile, "Done deal, and I'm delivering it tomorrow!"

18

Preset for a Purpose

Thousands of radio presets—and one life changed.

"So is my word that goes out from my mouth: It will not return to me empty, but will accomplish what I desire and achieve the purpose for which I sent it" (Isaiah 55:11).

I was in my eighteenth year of selling cars. Each car I sold continued to have all the local Christian radio stations pre-set on the dial. This was close to 6,000 cars. I often hoped that someday, just one person would make all that effort worth it.

As I previously mentioned, many times when Linda would park our lease turn-ins in the staging area, she would tell me that Christian music was playing on the radio. That always put a smile on my face, but I was hoping for a bigger testimony.

I had been with Hines Park Ford for almost 3 years by this time when a young lady brought her car in for an oil change. As she waited for her car, she walked past the customer service lounge, through the showroom, and over to my desk.

"Mr. Thomas," she said, "you probably don't remember me, but one year ago, you sold me a new car. Since that time, I had fallen away from the Lord. But yesterday, one of the Christian stations you had programmed on my radio brought me back to the Lord. I just wanted to say thank you!"

I thanked her right back and expressed to her how much her testimony meant to me. This made it worth all the times I had set those radio dials.

19

The Van God Sent

When an unexpected voice told me to check the used car lot.

My sheep hear my voice, and I know them, and they follow me (John 10:27).

It's always exciting as a car salesperson to have your desk phone ring!

"Hines Park Ford. This is Gaylord. Can I help you?"

"Hi Gaylord. This is Rocky Barra."

"Hi Pastor Rocky. How are you doing?"

"I'm doing fine. I am looking for a twelve-passenger club wagon for the church. I am starting a new ministry, and this would be ideal because the driver won't need a chauffeur's licence like he would for a fifteen-passenger van."

I had sold him a fifteen-passenger van five years prior at McDonald Ford. His church was thirty miles away, and he had more than five Ford dealerships closer to him, yet he was calling me. He told me that the church board had approved no more than $30,000 for the vehicle.

I had never seen a twelve-passenger van, but I set out to look for one and found three that were at a dealer in Columbus, Ohio. I called up their manager, and they told me that with the $1,500 rebate, the invoice would be $29,000.

Oh my. I could save Pastor Rocky's Church $1,000! I was so excited, I raced down to Rebecca, my sales manager, and asked if I could sell a dealer trade out of Columbus at invoice. I explained that it was for a church and that I knew the pastor. I said Linda and I would get the unit, so there would not be any extra expenses. She gave me the okay, and I couldn't get back to my desk fast enough.

As I started dialing Rocky, an audible voice said, "Check the used car lot!"

I thought, *Could there really be a twelve-passenger van on our used car lot?*

I ran to the window and saw only a delivery van, which had no windows. I was puzzled because I was sure I had heard clearly from the Lord. But I went back to the phone and started to dial Rocky; however once again I heard an audible voice say, "Check the used car lot!"

Since that was the second message, I thought I needed to dig deeper. So, I went to Dave—the most knowledgeable used car salesperson on the floor. He told me that there was no such van on the lot. I insisted there had to be one. His response was, "You and I have worked here at Hines Park Ford for three years, and there has never been an eight- or twelve-passenger Club Wagon on our lot.

I returned to my desk with my head down, disappointed. On my way back, a prior customer asked me a question about a car I had sold him. As I was talking to him, Dave came running toward me and said, "You're not going to believe this, but on the other side of the delivery van, there's a club wagon."

I ran to check it out. Sure enough! It was a white Club Wagon, and it looked new. I counted the seats. You guessed it: twelve.

I checked the odometer and found it had 17,000 miles on it. Posted in yellow paint was the van's year, and it was the same as we were selling new! I asked the used car manager where it came from, and he said he had purchased it at a used car auction the previous day. I could sell it for $19,000.

I said, "Sold!"

I called up Pastor Rocky and told him that I found three new ones in Ohio for $29,000. However, the Lord just dropped one out of the sky. It was used but the same year and only had 17,000 miles on it. The best part was that I could sell it for $19,000, saving the church $10,000.

Pastor Rocky replied, "Gaylord, put my name on it. I don't have it approved yet, but I'll be there first thing in the morning to purchase it."

As of this writing, that van has been serving the church for 18 years!

20

The Orange Mustang

The unforgettable test drive of a very special Mustang.

"Whatever you do, work at it with all your heart, as working for the Lord" (Colossians 3:23).

In our sales training, we learned the importance of presenting ourselves well—even after losing two or three sales in a row. Without training on handling rejection, you might greet the next potential customer with body language or an attitude that says, "You don't want to buy a car from me." You may not say it, but your body language will show it. You have to greet everyone as if you've just had three sales in a row—enthusiastic, upbeat, and positive. That next customer will take a liking to you because you're a winner.

On a cold Michigan morning in March, our dealership received a 2006 Parnelli Jones Saleen Mustang—one of only 500 produced.

Wow, what a car! We were one of only 500 Ford dealerships to receive this very special vehicle. It came only in Grabber Orange with black racing stripes and was so exclusive that it had a plaque signed by Steve Saleen and Parnelli Jones on the dash.

For the car buffs: It featured a Saleen-built 400 hp high-compression 302ci (5.0L) three-valve V8 with forged internal components and a functional shaker hood scoop. With its Tremec five-speed manual transmission, it could go from 0 to 60 mph in 4.5 seconds and run the quarter mile in 12.5 seconds. The car rode on a Saleen-tuned suspension with 19-inch wheels wrapped in Pirelli P Zero tires, and a 1970-style wing. The interior featured custom performance seats and a unique steering wheel. The sticker price was around $65,000—about $4,500 more than a Mustang GT. The commission would be double that of selling a Mustang GT.

When I saw the car, the Lord immediately brought to my mind a customer I had worked with about six years earlier—a man who loved specialty cars. I gave him a call, and he said he'd be right out.

He arrived quickly and was impressed with the specs, though he was no stranger to Saleen Mustangs.

I offered him a test drive. Normally, the dealership was cautious with cars like that, so I had to go along with him. When my Sales Manager asked why I was taking it out, I told him my customer was serious and eager.

My customer pulled onto the expressway ramp. Suddenly, we were at 60 mph in what felt like seconds, still in second gear, with three more gears to go. Wow! My head was glued to the seat. In third gear, we hit 90 mph before easing off at the next exit.

As we exited near the dealership, he turned onto a two-lane road posted at 35 mph and made a tight U-turn—without touching the brakes. I think my internal organs changed places.

I was more than happy to get back to the dealership.

As we stepped out of the car, I asked, "Do you want to purchase it?"

He replied, "No. It doesn't sound like a Mustang."

So, I pulled up a silver Mustang GT and had him take that for a drive. When he came back, he said, "I want a Mustang GT in red."

I asked what he planned to do with the car. He told me he would ship it to his home in Arizona, where he spent one month each winter.

I explained that the Mustang GT would be fine for that kind of use. However, the GT will depreciate each year while the Saleen would likely increase in value by about $1,000 a year in Arizona.

He replied, "Okay, order me a red Parnelli Jones."

I told him they only came in orange.

He shook his head and said he didn't want orange, so he'd take the red GT instead.

As I walked inside, I turned around and told him to take some time and really consider how much the orange Parnelli Jones might appreciate while sitting in his garage in Arizona.

About thirty minutes later, he called me and said, "Park the Saleen inside. I'll pick it up Monday and pay cash."

21

Finishing Strong

How God helped me end my career exactly the right way.

I have fought the good fight, I have finished the race, I have kept the faith" (2 Timothy 4:7).

It was the first week of July 2007. I had just finished a record month in June, selling and delivering more cars than ever before—and I had even bought myself a Mustang convertible.

As I walked across the showroom floor one day, I heard God speak to me in an audible voice, telling me that the owner of Hines Park Ford was going to congratulate me on my sales performance. Sure enough, not long after, the owner called me into his office and asked me to sit down. He did exactly what the Lord had just told me would happen—he congratulated me on my sales.

Then I sensed the Lord telling me that this would be the perfect time to ask for a favor.

I told him how much Linda and I loved working there. However, we were both at retirement age—sixty-five—and with Social Security and a small pension, we didn't really need to work anymore. And Michigan winters can be tough on a person (not to mention, the winter months were usually lower on sales).

I said, "We would really hate to leave, so I'll make you a deal. If you will allow us to take the slow months off each year—January, February, and March—Linda and I will give you two more years."

He replied, "Done!"

Since that went so well, I added that we would also like a week off in the spring and another in the fall so we could visit the Smoky Mountains.

He smiled and said, "Done!"

Later that day, my sales manager, Rebecca, told me that if anyone asked for me and purchased a car during those three months, I would still receive half the commission.

I love being a King's kid!

Final Reflection

A Life of Faith on the Showroom Floor

Looking back over all those years on the showroom floor, I can see God's hand in everything.

He guided me to the right dealerships, brought the right customers through the door, and even helped me when I made mistakes. Selling cars was never just about selling cars.

It was about people.

Every handshake was a new friendship.

Every delivery was an opportunity to encourage someone.

And every car radio I preset with Christian stations was a small prayer that God might touch someone's life.

I never imagined as a young boy driving my pedal car that one day I would spend my life doing something I loved so much.

Linda and I retired and moved to the Smokey Mountains. I like to say I'm on vacation for life! The Lord has blessed us with a wonderful church, and dear friends. I love sharing testimonies of the Lord's work with friends and strangers alike. I may have retired from car sales, but we never retire from the kingdom of God.

God truly does give us the desires of our hearts. And I can honestly say that through all those years…

I have *loved* being a King's kid.

www.ingramcontent.com/pod-product-compliance
Lightning Source LLC
LaVergne TN
LVHW011031110826
845149LV00015B/3375

* 9 7 8 1 9 5 9 5 4 7 0 9 9 *